BRIGHT SHENG

T0088341

MY OTHER SONG

FOR PIANO

ED 4625
First Printing: June 2017

ISBN: 978-1-4950-9532-0

G. SCHIRMER, Inc.

DISTRIBUTED BY

HAL•LEONARD®
7777 W. BLUEMOUND RD. P.O. BOX 13819 MILWAUKEE, WI 53213
www.halleonard.com
www.musicsalesclassical.com

MY OTHER SONG was commissioned by Music Accord, Inc.
expressly for pianist, Yefim Bronfman

The world premiere was presented on 20 May 2007
at the Rose Theater of Lincoln Center in New York
by the Chamber Music Society of Lincoln Center
Yefim Bronfman, piano

A recording is availble on NAXOS 9.70235
Peter Serkin, piano

Composer's Note

In 1990, after eight years in the United States, I wrote my first work for solo piano, entitled *My Song*, commissioned for Peter Serkin. At the time, my primary compositional concentration was to develop a melodic and harmonic style within the boundaries of Chinese folk music, which is mostly in pentatonic modes, and contemporary Western Classical music. As a result, all four movements in *My Song* were either based on existing Chinese folk tunes or written in that style. Seventeen years later, I was asked by another virtuoso pianist friend, Yefim Bronfman, to write a work for solo piano. After the passing of so many years, I was intrigued to see if there would be any change in my compositional writing style. I therefore entitled the new suite *My Other Song*.

There are four movements in the composition, the first three of which are brief and provide contrast in character. The theme of the last movement, the longest, is based on a Buddhist chant heard at the wake for my mother in February 2005.

—Bright Sheng

duration circa 20 minutes

Information on Bright Sheng and his works is available at:
www.musicsalesclassical.com

to Yefim

MY OTHER SONG

I

Bright Sheng

2

II

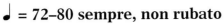 = 72–80 sempre, non rubato

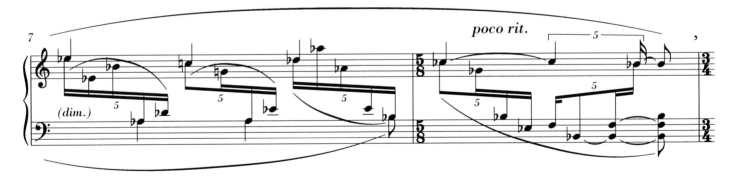

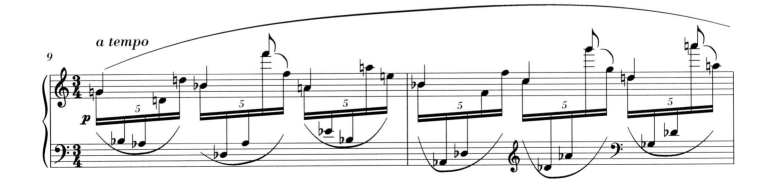

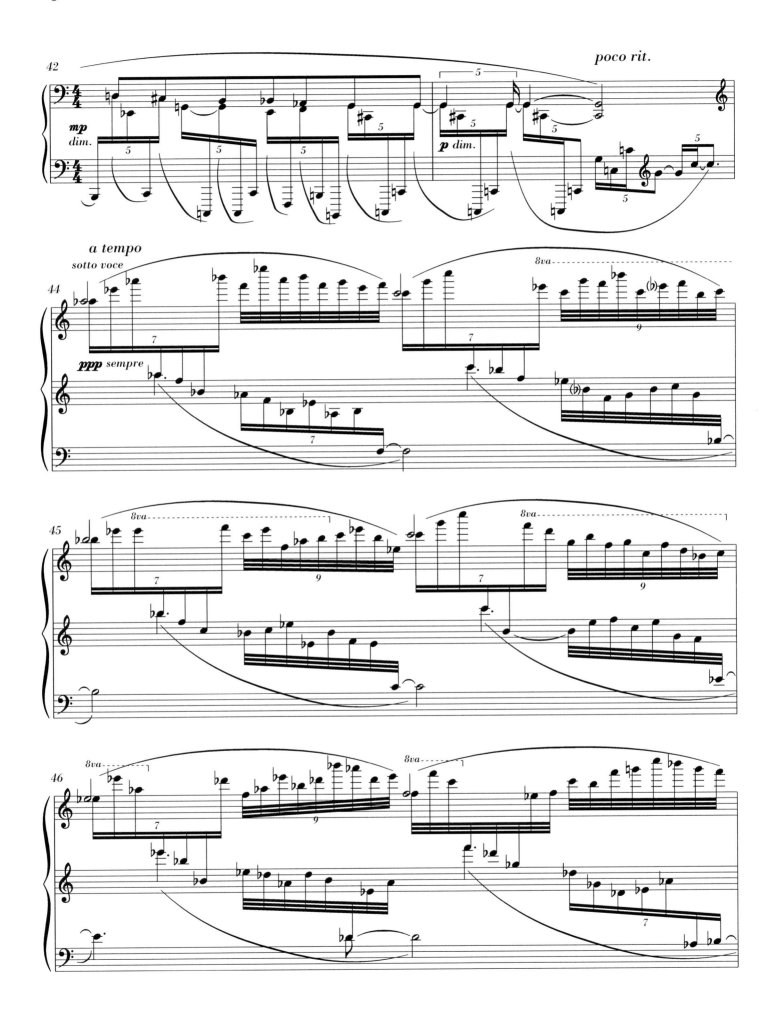

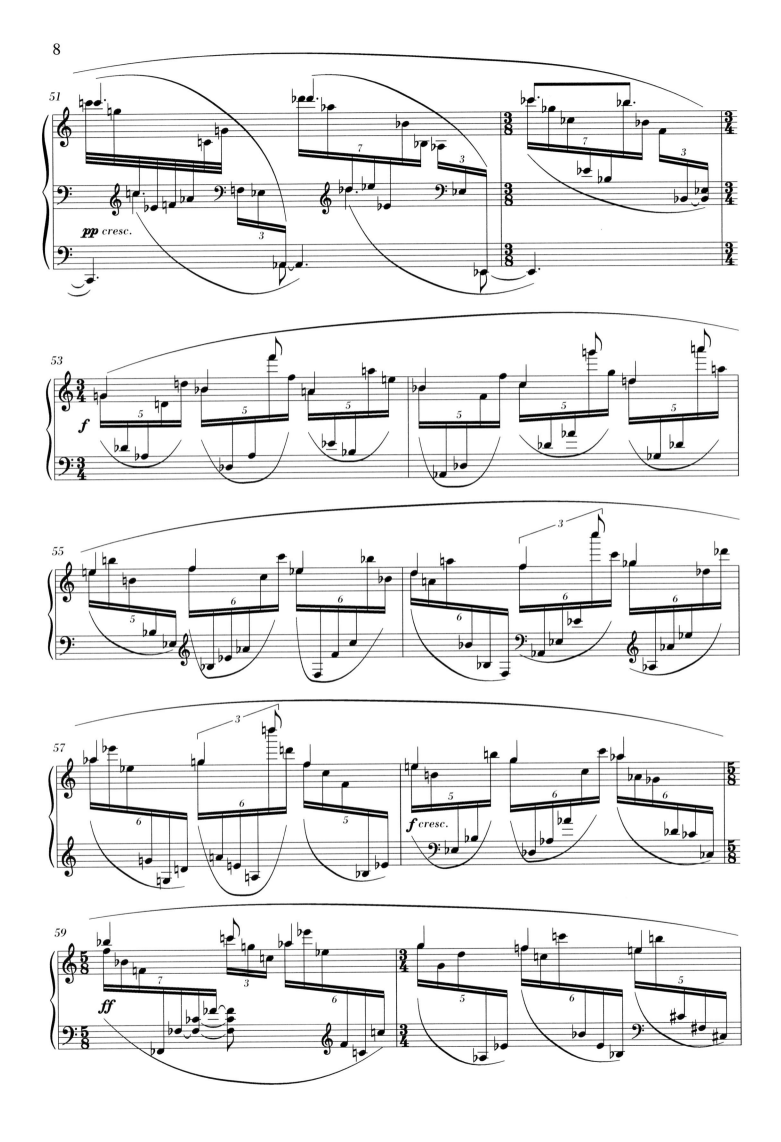

III

Prestissimo (♩ = 132–152)

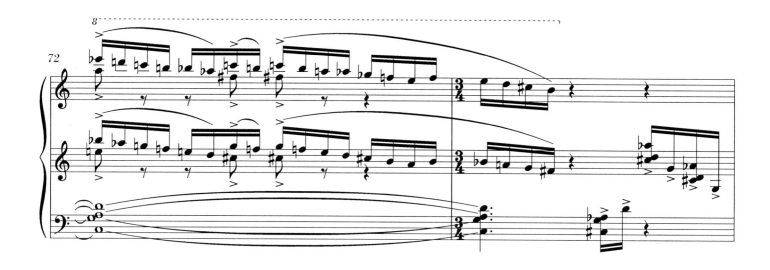

Slow funeral march   IV

22

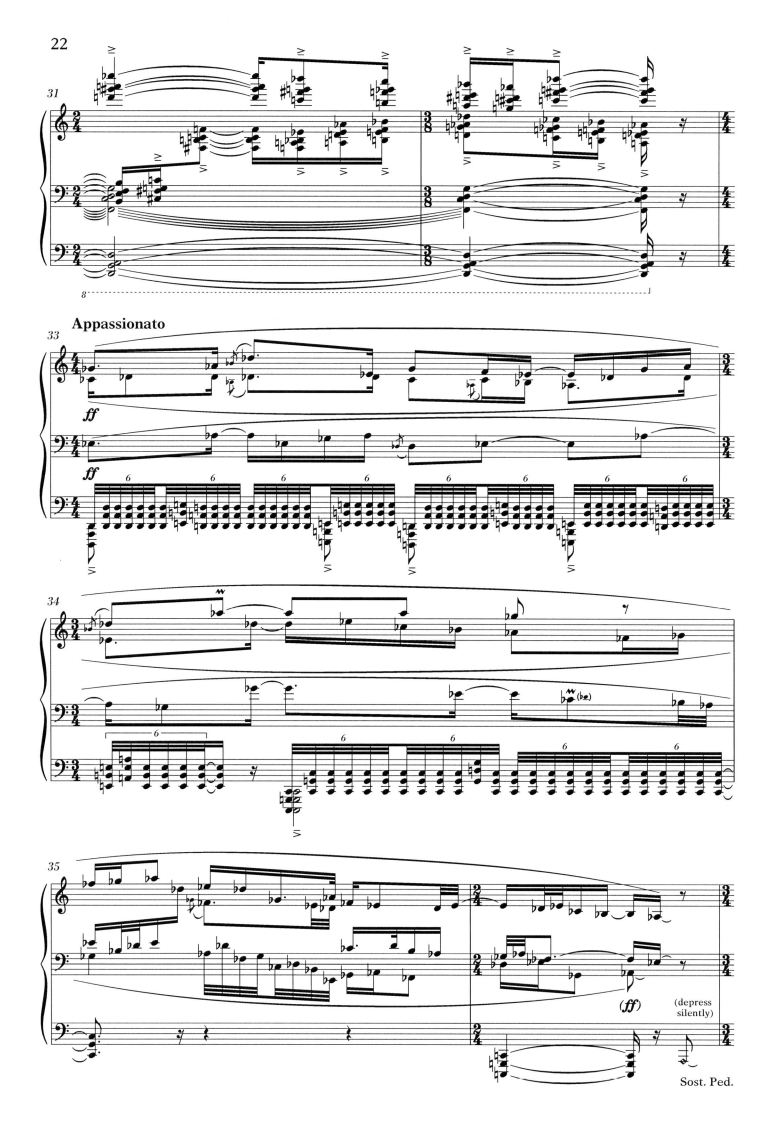

Appassionato

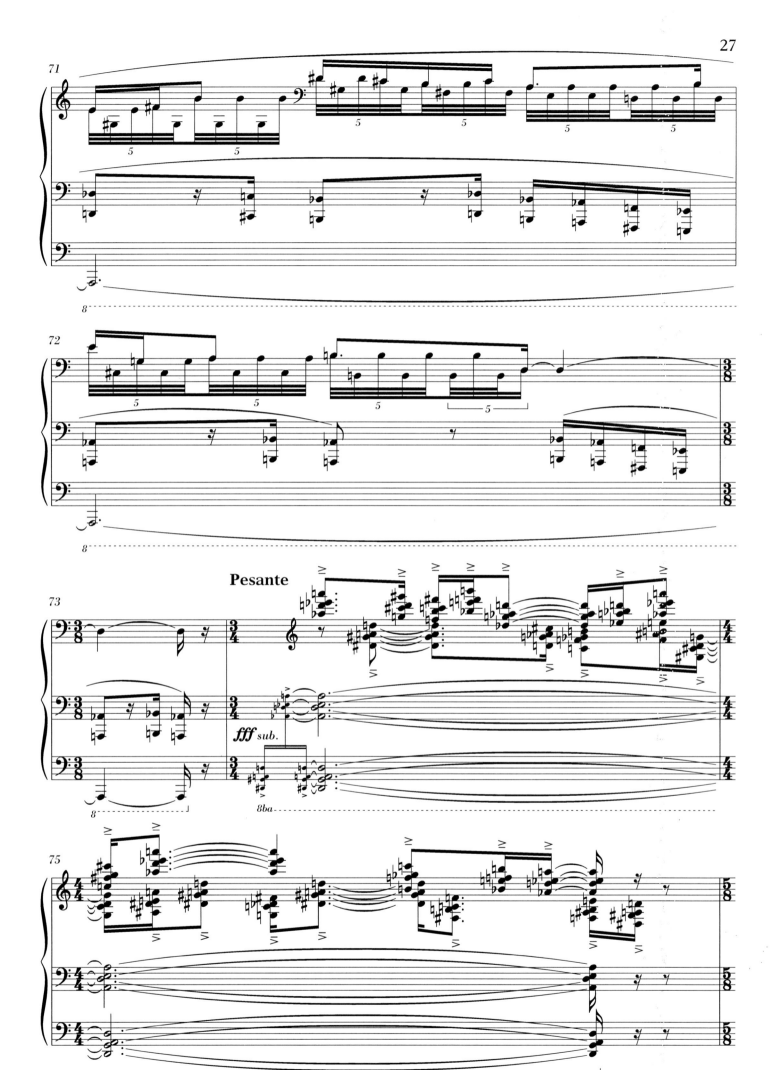

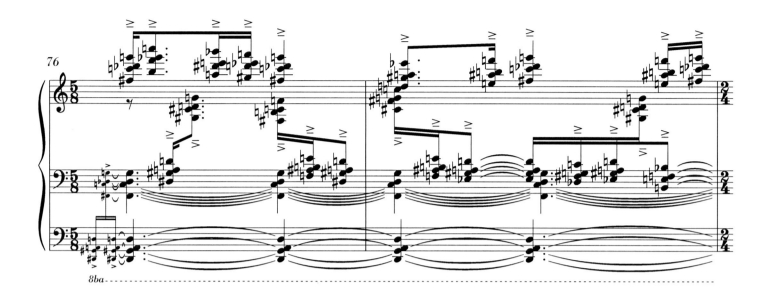

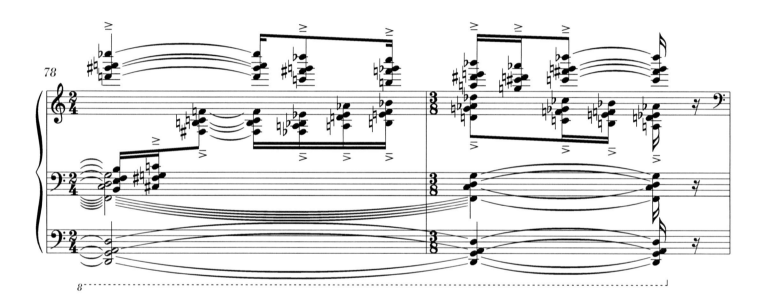

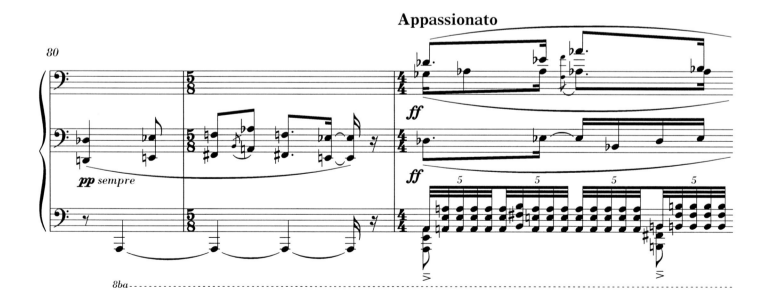